Safety

Kate Purdie

WAYLAND

First published in 2009 by Wayland
Copyright © Wayland 2009

Wayland, 338 Euston Road, London NW1 3BH
Wayland Australia, Level 17/207 Kent Street, Sydney, NSW 2000

Produced for Wayland by Calcium
Design: Nick Leggett and Paul Myerscough
Editor: Sarah Eason
Picture research: Maria Joannou
Consultant: Sue Beck MSc, BSc
Commissioning Editor for Wayland: Jennifer Sanderson
Printed in China

Acknowledgements
The publisher would like to thank the following for permission to reproduce photographs:
Alamy Images: Angela Hampton Picture Library 25, Digital Vision/Marcelo Santos 7, Peter Titmuss
13; Corbis: Bloomimage 15, Tom Grill 8, Stephen Mallon/Flame 11; Getty Images: Altrendo images
24, Iconica 6, Istockphoto: Karen Town 14, Arne Trautmann 10, Shutterstock: Yuri Arcurs 26, 31,
Marilyn Barbone 22, Ellen C 29b, Stacey Lynn Brown 21, David Davis 27, Laurence Gough 9,
Angela Hawkey 17, Hugo Maes 18, Pelham James Mitchinson 5, Amy Myers 23, Pablonilo 19,
Isaiah Shook 4, Popescu Simona 16, Alexander Sysoev 20, Olga Vasilkova 1, 12.

Wayland is a division of Hachette Children's Books, an Hachette UK company.
www.hachette.co.uk

British Library Cataloguing in Publication Data
Purdie, Kate
Safety. - (Being healthy, feeling great)
1. Home accidents - Prevention - Juvenile literature
2. Accidents - Prevention - Juvenile literature
3. Risk - perception - Juvenile literature
I. Title
613.6

ISBN: 978 0 7502 5893 7

Contents

At home

Safety is something we all need to think about as we go through life. Knowing common-sense ways to stay safe in different situations is great, and makes you feel confident.

Home is somewhere you can relax and enjoy spending time with your family. There are lots of simple ways to ensure that you stay safe at home.

In the sitting room

On a cold winter's day, there is nothing cosier than curling up in front of a fire with a good book or watching a favourite television programme. You can stay safe near fires and heaters by making sure that you do not sit too close to them to avoid getting burned. Putting items, such as magazines or games, on top of heaters or lamps, or near candles, can cause a fire.

A fire can quickly take hold. It can be devastating and dangerous.

4

In the kitchen

A lot of things can go wrong in the kitchen, so being safe is important. As you get older, it is fun to help with preparing meals. Knives can be very sharp, so always take care when using them. Use a tray when you carry hot drinks or plates.

Electrical items, such as kettles, toasters and irons and microwaves, should always be handled carefully. If your hands are wet when you touch something electrical, you could get a nasty electric shock. Always ask an adult for help in the kitchen when using a cooker.

Home alone

Never let anyone into your house without your parents' or caregivers' permission. If someone comes to the door, ask to see their proof of identity.

Be prepared!

Keeping safe is often about being prepared. Having smoke alarms means that if there is a fire at home, you will be warned in good time. Working out a safety plan with your family means that everyone will know what to do if a fire occurs.

Ask your parents to check the smoke alarms in your home every week.

Medicines and cleaning products

Medicines and cleaning products are found in all homes. While medicines and other products may be important, they can be dangerous if they are not used properly. Many medicine and cleaning bottles have safety caps to stop young children opening them. Part of being safe is knowing how to handle these products properly.

Medicines

Medicines come in many forms – as pills, creams, syrups, sprays and drops. You can buy some medicines in shops. Others need a prescription from a doctor. Wherever a medicine comes from, it needs to be taken with care. It can be harmful to use medicines that are not meant for you, or if you are not ill. If you take the wrong amount of medicine, or take it at the wrong time or in the wrong way, it may not work.

Taking medicine incorrectly could make you feel worse. This is why it is a good idea to take medicines with help from a parent or caregiver. Make a note of when you take the medicine and when you need to take it again. This will help you to get it right.

Always try to take your medicine with help from an adult.

It is great to help with housework. Take care when using cleaning products.

Cleaning products

All homes need to be kept clean. Furniture needs polishing, windows need washing and bathrooms need cleaning regularly – that is just for starters! Cleaning may be a chore, but a clean house is pleasant to live in and can help us to stay healthy.

People often use creams, soaps and sprays to make cleaning easier. These products should be used carefully. Accidentally spraying products into your eyes or spilling them onto your skin can make them sting or burn. Many cleaning products are poisonous and should never be swallowed. Some products release a poisonous gas if they are mixed together, and it is dangerous to breathe this in.

Amazing fact

In the UK, about 20 children die from suspected poisoning from household products every year.

At school

School is a place for learning and spending time with friends. Because there are so many people in a school, there are simple rules to help everyone to stay safe. For example, you are probably not allowed to run inside the school building. This rule helps to prevent accidents caused by falling over, or bumping into people or furniture. If you think about why rules exist, and you understand them, it makes it easier to follow them. If everyone follows the school rules, school will be much safer.

Go to school

Parents and caregivers need to know that children are safely at school. If you have to miss school – if you are ill, for example – school staff need to be told. That way, a responsible adult knows at all times where you are. For the same reason, whenever you are at school, it is important to stay within the school grounds at all times.

Always do what your teacher tells you to while on a school trip.

Healthy Hints

Fire drill

All schools have a plan, so that students and staff know what to do if a fire breaks out. Behave sensibly during a fire drill.

Paying attention

There are often rules at school about paying attention to teachers and other staff. Sometimes, staff need to tell you something important, such as how to use equipment in lessons. If you do not listen, you could hurt yourself. For example, in a gym class listen to the gym teacher and follow his or her instructions.

Keeping tidy

Many schools also have rules about keeping tidy. Students are often expected to put all equipment and books away when they have finished, and to put any litter in bins.

These rules help to keep schools safe and tidy. Accidents, such as students or teachers tripping over, can happen when objects or litter are in their way. Some types of litter can also attract rats and other pests, which can cause illness.

Laboratory equipment should always be used carefully and under instruction from a teacher.

Pedestrian safety

Pedestrians often walk in places where there is traffic, such as cars, lorries, motorbikes and bicycles. These sorts of vehicles can cause accidents – and even death. You need to take lots of care to make sure you stay safe when you are out walking. Try to always make sure an adult walks with you as often as you can.

Pavements

Most roads or streets have pavements for pedestrians to walk on. People should always stay on the pavement, away from the kerb. If there is a lot of traffic or if it is getting dark, it is best to walk in single file. In some places, there may not be a pavement. In this case, it is safest to walk on side of the road that faces the oncoming traffic. That way, you can see vehicles in good time – they will be able to see you, too.

Take care when walking on rough paths – you can easily trip over loose stones.

Amazing fact

Most children under nine cannot judge how fast vehicles are going or how far away they are.

Crossing the road

Following these road safety rules is the best way to stay out of danger when crossing the road. First of all, find a safe place to cross. You should be able to see the traffic clearly in both directions. If you can, use a pedestrian crossing – but still follow steps 1–3!

1. Stand on the pavement, not too close to the kerb. Look in every direction to see if any vehicles are coming. Listen carefully, too – sometimes, you can hear traffic that you cannot yet see.

2. Wait until it is safe to cross the road. If there is any traffic, let it pass. When you cross, there should be no traffic – or plenty of time to cross before any traffic reaches you. If you are not sure, wait! It is not worth taking any risks.

3. As you cross the road, keep looking and listening out for traffic until you reach the other side. Always walk straight across the road. Do not run, because you could trip and fall.

Try to use a pedestrian crossing whenever you cross the road.

Safe cycling

Cycling is great for everyone. It keeps you fit and healthy – and it is fun! Because there can be a lot of other traffic on roads, do all you can to stay safe when you are on your bicycle. Try to make sure an adult cycles with you.

Check your gear!

Before you set off, check that your bike is safe to ride. Do the tyres need fixing or pumping up? Have you checked that your brakes and lights are working properly? Are you wearing the right clothing? Cycle helmets are vital. Helmets can prevent head injuries – and save your life – if you fall off your bike or are knocked over. Reflective clothing, such as arm bands, makes you more visible on the road.

On the road

Cyclists should cycle in single file on the edge of the road, near the pavement. Use cycle lanes if possible. They keep cyclists separate from other vehicles, which is safer.

Make sure the straps of your cycle helmet are securely fastened.

Road safety

Like pedestrians, cyclists need to be very aware of road safety. They need to be able to hear, as well as see, other traffic. Using headphones or a mobile telephone when cycling is very dangerous. Cyclists need to stay completely focused on the road.

Other road users need to know what cyclists are planning to do. Whenever you set off, or turn left or right, look behind you and use the correct arm signals. Always check that it is safe to go. If you are not sure, wait! It can sometimes be safer to get off your bike and walk.

Traffic lights and road signs apply to cyclists, as well as to drivers. You can learn about the meaning of road signs in books and on the Internet.

Avoid cycling on the road without an adult.

Healthy Hints

Cycling courses

Do a cycling course to learn how to cycle safely. It will teach you all you need to know, including the correct arm signals to use.

On transport

We all use transport at some time. People use cars or trains for a family holiday. Children often go on school trips by coach. As you get older, you may be allowed to catch the bus into town with friends. Whenever you use different types of transport, you need to do what you can to stay safe.

In the car

It is safer to get into and out of a car using the door that is next to the pavement. Inside the car, everyone should use either a seatbelt or a child booster seat, depending on their age and height. In many countries, such as the United Kingdom and USA, this is the law. The law is there for everyone's safety.

Passengers should always allow the driver to concentrate on driving. If passengers are too noisy, it can be distracting. Opening the door when a car is moving is highly dangerous. It is safest not to touch the door or lean out of the car window.

Seatbelts and child booster seats can save lives.

14

On the bus or coach

Whilst waiting for a bus or coach, the safest place to stand is on the pavement, away from the kerb. Coaches often have seatbelts. If you sit upstairs, be careful when using the steps – especially if the bus is moving!

On the train

Stay away from rail tracks and from the edge of platforms at stations. Trains move very fast and if someone slipped onto the track, it would be almost impossible for a train to stop in time.

There is often a gap between the train platform and the train's steps. When getting on and off a train, you must be careful not to catch your foot in the gap. On the train, stay sitting down or stand holding on tightly.

Stay safe by standing behind the yellow line at train stations.

Healthy Hints

Where to?

If you are travelling anywhere without an adult, write down all you need to remember about your journey, such as bus times and where to get off the bus.

Near water

Playing in water – at the pool or sea, or in a lake or river – can be a lot of fun, especially on a hot day. However, you need to play safely, otherwise things can quickly go wrong.

Lakes and rivers

In winter, it may get cold enough for ponds and rivers to freeze over. These make tempting ice rinks, but it can be hard to know how thick the ice is and how much weight it can to take. You could find yourself plummeting into icy cold water.

This frozen lake can hold the weight of this duck, but maybe not you!

Healthy Hints

Swim safely

Always go swimming with an adult, who can help you to spot any dangers or help you if you get into difficulties.

Spot the dangers

Before getting into water, it is wise to check it out. How deep is it? Is there anything on the bottom that could injure you, such as broken glass? Is it easy to get out of the water? If you are at all unsure, you should not get in. It is best to go to a swimming pool or a beach with a lifeguard.

At the pool and beach

You should always take care when jumping or diving into swimming pools. If the water is not deep enough, you could seriously hurt yourself. If there are other people in the pool, you could hurt them, too. Being sensible in the pool will help to keep you safe.

At some beaches, there are special flags and notices that warn people about any possible dangers. Ignoring these can put people in danger. Beaches and swimming pools often have lifeguards to keep people safe, and it is important to follow their advice.

No-go areas

You should never swim in weirs, canals or quarries. The water there could be dangerously deep and cold. In a canal, you could also be hit by a passing boat.

Always check what the different coloured flags on the beach mean before you swim in the sea.

Out and about

It is fun to be out and about, especially with your friends. You may be allowed to walk to school without an adult or to go to the park to play with friends, so it helps to know what you can do to feel confident and stay safe.

Keep people informed

When you go out, make sure a responsible adult knows where you are going, who you are going with and what time you will be home. If, for any reason, you are late home, they will be able to find you. Remember to call to let them know if you are going to be home late.

Know what to do in an emergency

If you get lost, you could ask a police officer or a traffic warden for directions. Or go into a shop you know and ask an assistant for help. If you can, carry a mobile telephone with you so you can call home if you get into any trouble. But remember to keep the mobile out of sight in a safe place.

Stray dogs can carry fleas and diseases, so it is best not to touch them.

Always check that park equipment is not broken before you use it.

Know your route

If you are going out, you should always know exactly where you are going. Working out the safest route to school, the shops or to a friend's house is a good idea. You should never go out alone when it is dark.

Playing safe

Never play in places that may be dangerous, such as building sites, empty buildings or alleys. Places may not be as safe as they look.

For example, a playground might have broken swings. Do not touch any broken glass, needles or rubbish – it could be very dangerous.

If you see stray dogs or other animals, it is best not to touch them. You cannot tell if they are carrying diseases or if they might bite you. If you see a dog being taken for a walk and you want to stroke it, ask the owner first. Some dogs are not very comfortable meeting strangers!

In the sunshine

Sunshine makes you feel good! You can do things that are harder to do when it is cold or raining, such as spending the day in the park and having a picnic. The sun is really strong, and it can burn you – even through clouds. Sunburn can be very sore, so you should always take care to protect your skin.

Keeing out of the sun

The sun is at its strongest between 11am and 3pm. To avoid burning, it is best to stay out of the sun during these times. You could play indoors for a while, or go into a shady area, if you can find one. Covering up with a T-shirt, and protecting your head and eyes with a hat and sunglasses is a good idea.

Sitting in the shade when the sun is at its hottest gives you extra protection.

Protect your skin

Always use a sunscreen with an SPF of at least 15 to make sure your skin is properly protected.

Using sunscreen

Protect your skin from the sun's strong rays with sunscreen. When you are outdoors, you should regularly apply sunscreen to your body. Any skin that is not covered with clothes should be covered with sunscreen.

All sunscreens have a Sun Protection Factor (SPF) rating. This tells you how much the sunscreen will block the sun's strong rays, called UVA and UVB rays. Choose a sunscreen that protects you from both UVA and UVB rays.

You need to protect your skin with a generous amount of sunscreen. The sunscreen needs to be rubbed lightly into the skin. You should put sunscreen on about 15–20 minutes before going out in the sun, then reapply it at least every two hours. Waterproof sunscreen keeps protecting your skin if you go swimming or play in a pool. However, you will still need to reapply each time you come out of the water.

Apply sunscreen to every part of your body that is out in the sun.

During sport

Doing sport keeps people fit and healthy, and is a good way to make friends. There are lots of sports to choose from, such as football, netball, martial arts and badminton.

To get the most out of your chosen sport, it is a good idea to get help from an expert. You might have lessons at school, or go to a club after school or at the weekend. During lessons, you can find out about the rules of the game, how to improve your skills and what you need to do to stay safe.

Preventing injury

The correct clothes and footwear help people to move comfortably during sport. Wearing protective items – such as shin pads when playing football – is essential. Before you start your activity, take time to check any equipment, to make sure that it is working properly.

The right help and equipment helps you to stay safe during sport.

Follow the rules

Many sports have a referee to help players to keep to the rules. Always listen to the referee, or to your sports teacher. And always stick to the rules of the game, so everyone stays injury-free!

Looking after your body

Doing sport uses up energy, so your body needs to be ready before you start. If you exercise just after eating, you may feel heavy and unwell. If you exercise on an empty stomach, you might feel dizzy and sick. It is best to eat a healthy meal at least one hour before exercising.

When you do sport, you get hot and you sweat. It is important to replace the liquid you lose from your body when you sweat. Always drink water before, during and after exercise.

Healthy Hints

Eat healthily

Try to eat a healthy, balanced diet. Keep your body healthy for doing sport.

Always try to listen to your coach when you play sport.

23

Stranger danger

A stranger is someone you do not know. Most strangers are nice, normal people, but others are not.

It is not possible to tell if someone is good or bad, just by looking at them. So, it is usually safer to avoid contact with strangers, especially if you are on your own.

Two's company

It is much safer to be with other people when you are out and about. A stranger is much less likely to come up to you if you are with someone else, or in a busy place. If you do go out alone, you should always let an adult know where you are going and when you will be home.

Taking any gifts, such as sweets, from a stranger should always be avoided.

No, no, no!

Never, ever go anywhere with a stranger. It could be very dangerous. Never get in a stranger's car, accept anything from them or do anything they ask you to do. They may try to persuade you in different ways. They may offer you a lift on a cold day. Strangers may offer you sweets. They may say that they need your help, perhaps to find their puppy. *Remember – the answer is always: 'No, no, no!'.*

Yell, run, tell

If anyone frightens you in any way, you need to shout and get away quickly. Yell loudly, 'No!' or 'Stop!'. Then run as fast as you can. Run somewhere you know is safe, such as your home or school, or to a shop. Tell someone you can trust, such as a parent or police officer, what has happened.

Never, ever accept a lift from someone you do not know.

Healthy Hints

Who can help?

Discuss with your parents or caregivers who it is safe to go to for help. Police officers, nurses, paramedics and fire fighters may be strangers, but they will help you.

Internet safety

The Internet is a great source of information. There are lots of websites for you to surf. People use the Internet to stay in touch with friends, using e-mail and social networking sites. However, the Internet can be risky, if you do not know how to stay safe. You may come across websites and people who are dangerous. It is important to know how stay out of danger.

Agree rules

If you have the Internet at home, it is sensible to agree rules with your parents or caregivers about going online. Agree when you can use the Internet, how long for – and the safe sites you can visit. Always stick to what you have agreed, because this will help to keep you safe.

Keep it secret!

Keep your personal details secret. Never give out your full name, home address, telephone number, the name of your school or put photos of yourself on the Internet. Keep your passwords safe, too. You can never be sure who will look at information about you and try to contact you.

Using the Internet can be useful and fun, but make sure you always use it safely.

Often when you enter a chat room online, you are asked to give your age, sex and location. It is much safer to use a nickname and not to say exactly where you are.

Hoaxers

You may come across people you do not know on places such as social networking sites. Remember, these are strangers! Not everyone tells the truth on the Internet. Some people are hoaxers – you do not know who they really are.

It can be very dangerous to meet up with someone you have met online. If you want to meet someone, ask your parents or caregivers to go with you. Make sure you meet up in a place where there are lots of people.

Tell your parents or teacher if anything happens online that makes you feel uncomfortable, worried or upset.

Never give out your phone number online – a stranger may call you.

Who knows?

Your parents or caregivers can set sensible restrictions on your home computer so that you visit only safe websites online.

Healthy Hints

In an emergency

CONTACT 1:
TEL:
MOBILE:
Sam Smith
01297 44419
07968 3045

CONTACT 2:
TEL:
MOBILE:
Jane Summer
01297 45895
07802 54709

It is easy to stay safe most of the time. However, it is always sensible for everyone to know what to do if there is an emergency.

Your contact details

Learn your full name, your address and your telephone number. Then you can tell someone you trust, such as a police officer, if you need help.

Family and friends

Learn work and mobile telephone numbers for your parents or other caregivers. That way, you can contact them when you need to.

Learn telephone numbers for other people, such as your grandparents or a close family friend, in case you cannot get hold of your parents or caregivers. You could write the numbers on a tag, such as the one top right. Wear the tag at all times, so you always have the numbers to hand.

Know how to phone the emergency services

In the UK, dial 999 from any phone. In the USA, dial 911. You will be asked which emergency service you require. You will need to ask for the police, ambulance or fire service. If you are not sure, the operator will help you.

Answering questions

Answer any questions, for example, about where you are, the number you are calling from and what the emergency is. Remember to try to stay calm and to speak clearly. Never put the phone down until you are told to do so – you may forget to give the emergency services an important piece of information.

Quiz

Try the safety challenge!

1 It is a hot day and you fancy swimming in the local river. Do you:

a) Have a quick look and decide it is OK?
b) Ask your mum or dad to check it out with you to see if it is safe?
c) Jump straight in? What's the worst that could happen?

2 You find some of your mum's pills. Do you:

a) Give one to the dog?
b) Give them to your mum and ask her to put them in a safe place?
c) Try one; they look colourful and tasty?

3 There is no pavement for you to walk on. Do you:

a) Walk in the middle of the road?
b) Walk in single file, facing any traffic?
c) Try to get a lift from someone in a car?

4 A stranger asks you to help to find his puppy. Do you:

a) Call your friend, and both of you go with him?
b) Shout 'No!', and run somewhere safe to get help?
c) Get into his car – he looks like a nice person?

5 You are in a chat room talking to a new friend. She asks you for your mobile phone number and a photo. Do you:

a) Ask her for hers first?
b) Tell her that you do not give out personal information online. Then tell your mum or dad about it?
c) Find a photo of you looking at your best and post it online?

Answers

Mostly **bs**: Well done! You have learned a lot about how to stay safe in lots of different situations. Stay sharp by reading different books and websites that can give you even more information. Keep up the good work!

Mostly **as** or **cs**: You have some way to go before you are safety smart. Remember, staying safe is not difficult; you just need to think about different situations so you can be prepared. Keep reading this book; it will give you lots of ideas! And talk to your parents or caregivers, too – they will be able to give you lots of advice.

Glossary

arm signals The movements made by a cyclist with the arm and hand, to let other road users know that they are planning to turn or stop.

chat room A part of the Internet where people use e-mail to discuss things with other people.

child booster seat A seat in a car that raises a child to a higher level.

electric shock A sudden, painful feeling when electricity goes through your body.

emergency services Organisations that deal with accidents and urgent problems, such as fire and crime.

fire drill When people practise what they should do to leave a building safely when there is a fire.

hoaxer Someone who deceives someone else.

kerb The edge of a pavement nearest the road.

law A rule made by the government.

lifeguard A person at a beach or swimming pool, whose job is to make sure that swimmers stay safe.

martial arts Traditional Japanese or Chinese sports such as karate and kung-fu.

operator A person whose job it is to receive phone calls and connect them to other numbers.

pedestrian crossing A marked place in a road where traffic must stop to allow people to cross.

poisoning Illness caused by a substance that can harm people if they eat or drink it.

prescription A note from a doctor to say which medicine someone needs.

seatbelt A belt that fastens around someone to hold them in their seat.

single file Walking with one person behind another.

smoke alarms Devices that make a loud noise when there is smoke.

social networking sites Places on the Internet, such as Facebook, where people chat to each other and exchange information.

staff People who work for an organisation.

sunscreen A lotion or cream you put on your skin to prevent it burning in the sun.

surf To spend time looking at lots of places on the Internet.

websites Places on the Internet that have information about a subject.

Find out more

Books

Keeping Healthy: Safety
Carol Ballard, (Wayland, 2004)

Safety First: In the Home
Ruth Thomson
(Franklin Watts, 2008)

Safety First: Near Water
Ruth Thomson
(Franklin Watts, 2008)

Safety First: On the Road
Ruth Thomson
(Franklin Watts, 2008)

Safety First: With Strangers
Helena Attlee
(Franklin Watts, 2008)

Know the Facts: Personal Safety
Judith Anderson
(Wayland, 2008)

Websites

A fun website with games about road safety.
www.hedgehogs.gov.uk/main/ main.html

Find out about how to cycle safely at:
www.bikeability.org.uk

This website is packed with information about staying safe when using the Internet.
www.kidsmart.org.uk

A confidential website and helpline for children who are in trouble and danger, and who need to talk. For free telephone help, dial 0800 1111.
www.childline.org.uk

Index